D0715515

capturing
MINDFULNESS

Your typical day is neither
beautiful nor ugly, good nor bad.

It's purely as you see it.

CAPTURING

MINDFULNESS

A guide to becoming present through photography

Written and photographed by Matthew Johnstone

ROBINSON

Constable & Robinson Ltd
55–56 Russell Square
London WC1B 4HP
www.constablerobinson.com

First published 2013 in Pan by Pan Macmillan Australia Pty Ltd, 1 Market Street, Sydney

This edition published in the UK by Robinson,
an imprint of Constable & Robinson Ltd, 2014

A copy of the British Library Cataloguing in Publication Data
is available from the British Library

ISBN: 978-1-47211-326-9 (paperback)
ISBN: 978-1-47211-345-0 (ebook)

1 3 5 7 9 10 8 6 4 2

Design by Matthew Johnstone

Printed in China

For My Mum

My heartfelt thanks to my supportive and loving family,
Fritha Saunders and everyone at Constable & Robinson,
To everyone at Curtis Brown UK & Sydney,
Pauline Kidd for lighting the fuse on this book,
to everyone who has given me advice and valuable feedback
and to life, for teaching me what's truly important.

Foreword

During the course of making of this book people asked what it was about; I'd explain I was creating a book about developing mindfulness through photography. I often got that look of a dog that cocks its head when hearing a whistle somewhere in the distance.

For the average person *being in the moment*, *being present*, *becoming mindful* sound familiar but these are rarely practised or understood.

Modern-day society is generally about deadlines, ladder climbing, list ticking, friend and family wrangling, social networking, commuting and paying stuff off. All this 'busy-ness' can exact a hefty toll on our mental wellbeing and physical health. When overloaded and constantly stretched, our minds can become like an engine going at full throttle while in neutral. There's a lot going on yet we're not getting anywhere.

Mindfulness, simply put, is a heightened awareness or an act of paying close attention to what we are doing, where we are and what we're thinking; all without judgement or self-criticism, all with a slow and gentle intention.

Mindfulness doesn't solve life's problems but it's a proven, powerful psychological tool that helps us respond more calmly and with more self-awareness to what life throws at us. It's an effective coolant for our habitually stressed-out, self-sabotaging thinking styles.

Mindfulness can be practised during everyday activities such as eating, walking, listening, doing the dishes and driving. In my mind, one of the most wonderful and creative conduits to this often-elusive mind state is photography. I've been undertaking what I term a **photopresent** practice for over 15 years and next to meditation this is one of the greatest ways I can attain mindfulness in my day-to-day life. Photography, after all, is all about focusing and capturing **the moment**.

I am not a technical or a professional photographer but I am truly passionate about light, colour, composition and trying to see the world differently.

Photopresent for me is an excited quiet; I am hyper-aware of all that is around me; time slows, my mind and eye sharpen and there is nothing going on other than what is directly in front of me.

I truly hope the images within this book inspire you to go and find the space between a breath, to capture the tick before a tock or simply a moment when it's just you and the universe.

Matthew Johnstone

This may come as a surprise to some, but we are constantly surrounded by beauty and incredible moments.

The problem is we're often too busy,
self-absorbed and distracted to notice
what is going on right in front of us.

If we train ourselves to become more aware of the present moment, the ordinary can become **extraordinary.**

The busy can become ...

...calm.

We can find beauty
and inspiration where
they don't typically exist.

'Being in the moment' is easy to say yet tricky to do for the simple reason our mind is constantly being pulled in so many different and distracting directions.

Typically we are fast-forwarding to the future, rewinding to the past or operating purely on autopilot.
Hence the present 'moment' is often missed or lost.

To become reconnected with our lives, learning mindfulness is not only life-affirming but it's incredibly good for our mental health and wellbeing.

Mindfulness is not difficult, it merely requires a simple practice. One of the most satisfying and creative ways to harness the moment is through

photography

Life will inevitably pass us by but it needn't go unnoticed.

Let's call it being

Photography literally requires us to focus our attention on what's going on around us, right here and right now. Then we capture it.

A camera asks:
'What can you see that
no one else can?'

'What grabs you visually
that you can't fully explain?'

A camera allows us to steal
moments that are as
fleeting as our thoughts.

It encourages us to view the world in which we live

DIFFERENTLY

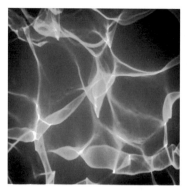

When we're present in the
current moment we are no
longer regretting the past
or fearing the future.
We're simply appreciating life's
beauty in all its complexity.

This in itself can bring
a certain calm and
peacefulness.

It really is quite

So where do we begin?

FROM NOWHERE TO NOW-HERE

Start with this moment **right here, right now** as you're holding this book.
Where are you? Are you in bed, on public transport, in a bookstore,
at the office, at the library, sitting in your favourite chair?

Are you alone? Are you surrounded by others? Are you with someone
special? Is it warm? Is it cold?

How are your thoughts: busy, vacant, foggy, agitated, tired, calm or happy?

Take a moment to centre yourself and then begin to mentally inhale
your surroundings – try not to fixate on anything in particular.
Try to pick up on the sounds, the smells and the light.
Study this truly unique scene before you.

As you look around, consciously slow, lengthen and deepen your breath.
A slow and easy breath results in a relaxed and open mind.

Although everything around you may be busy, tell yourself to 'slow down'.
Become a momentary epicentre of stillness.

Most importantly, try not to judge what you're feeling or seeing, simply
observe it. 'Acceptance' is the key ingredient to becoming more present.

We can't halt
our thoughts and
we can't stop time
but we can certainly
slow them down.

Now Look at the Book

Now bring your attention to the book itself. Feel its weight in your hand. What's the texture of the paper? What different hues of colour do you see? What light or shadow do you see bouncing off the page?

Choose a word; study that word until it ceases to be one.

Observe your hands holding the book: study your thumb; find something about your thumb you've never noticed before.

Become aware of the angle of your head, the nature of your breath, the touch of your clothing on your skin, your feet on the floor. Again, hit the internal pause button, slow everything right down to this very moment; wherever you may be in the world.

If you can, shut your eyes for a moment and turn up the volume on all your other senses.

This moment you are experiencing right now will never happen again. There are, however, an infinity of other moments just around the corner waiting to be captured with your awareness and your camera.

The past will remain
forever history.
The future will always
be tomorrow.

So why not learn to live in the

NOW?

Some quotes about mindfulness

'Mindfulness practice means that we commit fully in each moment to be present; inviting ourselves to interface with this moment in full awareness, with the intention to embody as best we can an orientation of calmness, mindfulness, and equanimity right here and right now.' Jon Kabat-Zinn,
Wherever You Go, There You Are: Mindfulness Meditation in Everyday Life

'Feelings come and go like clouds in a windy sky. Conscious breathing is my anchor.' Thich Nhat Hanh, *Stepping into Freedom: Rules of Monastic Practice for Novices*

'Realise deeply that the present moment is all you have. Make the NOW the primary focus of your life.' Eckhart Tolle,
The Power of Now: A Guide to Spiritual Enlightenment

Some quotes about photography

'Look and think before opening the shutter. The heart and mind are the true lens of the camera.' Yousuf Karsh

'Be still with yourself until the object of your attention affirms your presence.' Minor White

'Photography can only represent the present. Once photographed, the subject becomes part of the past.' Berenice Abbott

STILL. LIFE.

Thoughts to keep in MINDfulness

It could be said that people can lose entire moments by trying to photograph them: blowing out candles, first steps, the wedding kiss, a sunset, the portrait in front of a touristy vista, and so forth.

In itself, recording events for memory 'keepsakes' is not a bad thing but we can become so concerned about capturing what's happening or taking a good photograph that we actually miss the moment altogether. There may be physical proof that we were there, but often we're present and absent at the same time.

Being photopresent is something you set out to do with absolute intention.

It's a practice preferably done alone.

It's an 'eyes wide open' walking meditation.

It's not a time to worry about the technical aspects of photography.

It's a time to consciously slow down both mentally and physically and look at your world with a keen curiosity, as if seeing it for the first time.

Let the weight of the camera
in your hands be the
constant reminder to literally
keep focus on what's
happening right now,
no matter how busy.

*Never
is there a moment
when it's not
now-o'clock.*

Any time is a good time
to be **photopresent**, but often
the best results can be
found as the sun rises or sets.

The light, shadows and colours
are more interesting and it's
generally more peaceful.

An early bird gets the moment.

Develop a child's *eye*

If you're looking for inspiration, look to a child. Children have an amazing ability to be totally absorbed by what's in front of them. Their world view is uncluttered, funny, adventurous, beautiful and wonderfully simplistic. They are the masters of non-judgement. They take the world as they see it and express themselves accordingly.

Developing a **'child's eye'** can be helpful in your approach to taking photopresent images.

Practise being adventurous, playful and curious in the way you view your surroundings no matter how familiar.

Disregard how you 'should' take a photograph:

- **Lie on the ground.**
- **Shoot upside down, between your legs.**
- **Shoot out of focus.**
- **Be joyful. Be spontaneous. Be present.**
- **Pretend you don't care and you won't.**

Not only will life become more interesting but so will your photographs.

BECOME A TROPHY HUNTER

Sometimes becoming photopresent can be easier if you have something in mind you'd like to be present about; it could be a colour, words on a wall, a sunrise, nature, people, clouds, and so forth. Hunting an object of your desire can help you stay tuned into your surroundings.

You could also limit how many photos you take; this will force you to be more selective as well as more observant.

It's important to remember that being photopresent is about creating some time for yourself while heightening your awareness. You don't have to share your imagery with anyone and there is nothing to prove. It's not so much about the outcome; it's more the process and the practice.

Hopefully, over time, mindfulness should infuse your life and the way that you look and interact with it. With or without a camera, it's a wonderful thing to be aware of where you are, what you're doing and how you're feeling.

It's hard to be present all the time but with perseverance we can begin to take control of a wayward mind. We soon discover a calmer way of looking at the world and ourselves.

Someone once said that they thought my photographs had a sense of isolation or emptiness to them. There may be some truth in this but I see them more as having a sense of peace, stillness and tranquillity. I say this because it's what I feel when I take them and it's often what I feel when I look at and reflect on them.

To me they are reminders that stillness can be found, harnessed and appreciated in this frenetic, busy, socially networked world we inhabit. I truly hope they inspire you to become more aware of what you're doing, where you're doing it and that you too can slow the clock and truly *be here.*

'Don't count every hour in the day,
make every hour in the day count.'

Unknown

Final thoughts

1) I can't explain why, but one of the best residual and beneficial knock-on effects from a meditation practice is that you will naturally feel more present and engaged. It's a great springboard to being photopresent.

2) If you're going to use your smartphone while practising photopresent, switch it to 'Airplane Mode' so you're not tempted by everything a smartphone has to offer.

3) One way to focus more accurately on your surroundings is to keep a thin black piece of paper or card with a rectangle or square cut out of it. This can help frame whatever you may be looking at.
It's also bigger than a viewfinder or an LCD screen.

There is one included at the back of this book.

4) Go slow. Breathe slow. Be curious. Don't judge. See fresh. Take time.

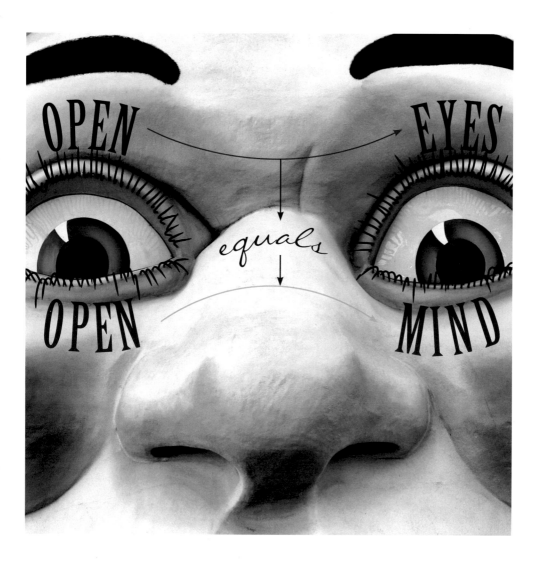

Recommended reading

Collard, Dr Patrizia (2013) *Journey into Mindfulness: Gentle Ways to Let Go of Stress and Live in the Moment,* Gaia Books Ltd

Dalai Lama (2010) *The Art of Happiness: A Handbook for Living,* Riverhead Books

Harris, Dr Russ (2008) *The Happiness Trap: How to Stop Struggling and Start Living,* Robinson Publishing

Kabat-Zinn, Jon (2004) *Wherever You Go, There You Are: Mindfulness Meditation for Everyday Life,* Piatkus

Tolle, Eckhart (2001) *The Power of Now: A Guide to Spiritual Enlightenment,* Hachette Publishing

Thich, Nhat Hanh (1999) *The Miracle of Mindfulness: An Introduction to the Practice of Meditation,* Beacon Press

About the author:

Matthew Johnstone
is an author, illustrator,
photographer, keynote speaker
and a passionate mental health /
wellbeing advocate and consultant.
He lives in Sydney, Australia,
with his wife and two children.

 www.matthewjohnstone.com.au

 drawnfromexperience

 www.facebook.com/DrawnFromExperience

Your mindful
photograph
here

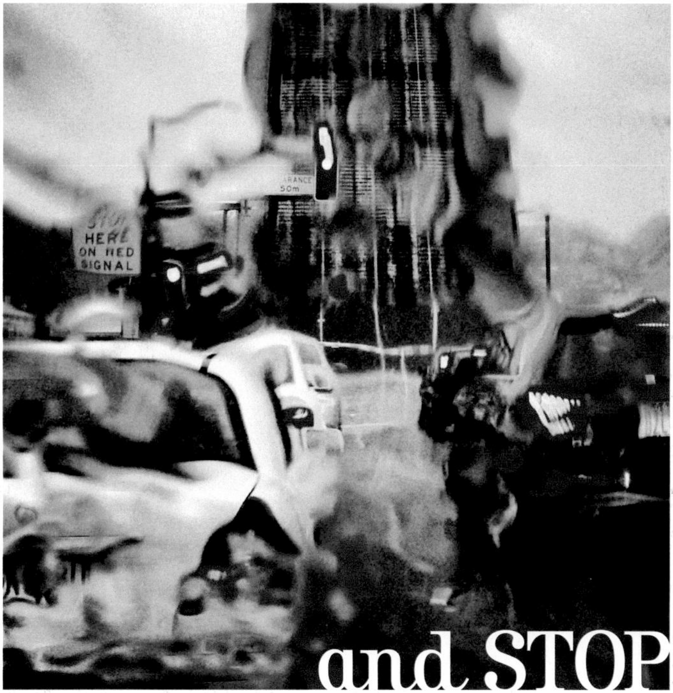
HERE
ON RED
SIGNAL
and STOP